ESSENTIAL LIBRARY OF
THE US MILITARY

★ THE US ★
NAVY

Essential Library

An Imprint of Abdo Publishing | www.abdopublishing.com

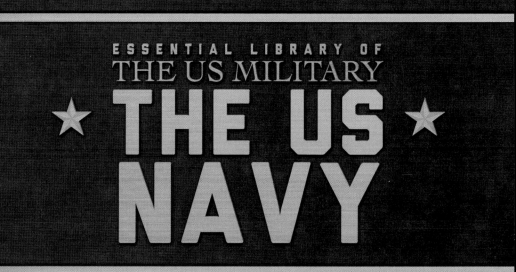

ESSENTIAL LIBRARY OF
THE US MILITARY

★ THE US ★
NAVY

BY SUSAN E. HAMEN

CONTENT CONSULTANT
JAMES C. BRADFORD
PROFESSOR OF HISTORY
TEXAS A&M UNIVERSITY

www.abdopublishing.com

Published by Abdo Publishing, a division of ABDO, PO Box 398166, Minneapolis, Minnesota 55439. Copyright © 2015 by Abdo Consulting Group, Inc. International copyrights reserved in all countries. No part of this book may be reproduced in any form without written permission from the publisher. Essential Library™ is a trademark and logo of Abdo Publishing.

Printed in the United States of America, North Mankato, Minnesota
042014
092014

Cover Photo: US Navy
Interior Photos: US Navy, 2, 18, 32, 35, 39, 40–41, 42, 47, 48, 50–51, 54, 56, 59, 63, 66–67, 70, 71, 73, 74, 76–77, 80, 83, 84–85, 87, 95, 96, 97, 100; Jacob J. Kirk/US Navy/AP Images, 6–7; Anat Givon/AP Images, 9; US Navy Photo/AP Images, 10; North Wind Picture Archives, 14–15; Edward Moran, 20; Thomas Chambers, 22; Lebrecht 3/Lebrecht Music & Arts/Corbis, 24–25; Library of Congress, 28; The Mariners' Museum, 30; Tim Page/Corbis, 37; Red Line Editorial, 45; US Air Force, 61; Patrick Semansky/AP Images, 90

Editor: Arnold Ringstad
Series Designer: Jake Nordby

Library of Congress Control Number: 2014932858

Cataloging-in-Publication Data

Hamen, Susan E.
 The US Navy / Susan E. Hamen.
  p. cm. -- (Essential library of the US military)
ISBN 978-1-62403-437-4
1. United States. Navy--Juvenile literature.   I. Title.
359.00973--dc23

2014932858

CONTENTS

CHAPTER ONE

SAILING TO THE RESCUE

The sunrise over Indonesia on December 26, 2004, promised a beautiful Sunday. Under blue skies that morning, people awoke and went about their normal routines. It was peak holiday season for tourists in Southeast Asia, and thousands of vacationers prepared for another day of fun and relaxation on the shores of the

The tsunami left few buildings standing in the hardest-hit areas.

Indian Ocean. No one had any reason to believe the day would turn into a nightmare of devastation.

At 7:59 a.m., an 8.9 magnitude earthquake occurred under the sea near Aceh, a northern province on the Indonesian island of Sumatra.[1] The quake generated a massive tsunami. Without warning, a tremendous and deadly wall of water reaching up to 50 feet (15 m) high fanned out and rolled across the ocean, crashing onto land and leaving a trail of destruction in its path.[2] More waves followed. Entire villages were wiped out. By the time the tsunami waves ended, nearly 230,000 people in 14 countries were dead or missing.[3] The tsunami waves had reached far enough inland that in many areas the roads were completely destroyed, cutting off survivors. Those who lived through the onslaught were left without food, clean water, and medical help as they struggled to pull injured survivors from the mountains of debris.

COMING TO THE RESCUE

The world watched in horror as news reports showed images and videos of the widespread destruction left behind by the tsunami. People around the world responded by donating much-needed money and supplies for the relief effort. But the US Navy was already on the way to offer aid to the tsunami victims.

When news of the earthquake and tsunamis reached US Pacific Command (PACOM) headquarters

"From our own experiences, we know that nothing can take away the grief of those affected by tragedy. We also know that Americans have a history of rising to meet great humanitarian challenges and of providing hope to suffering peoples. As men and women across the devastated region begin to rebuild, we offer our sustained compassion and our generosity, and our assurance that America will be there to help."[4]
—*President George W. Bush, January 3, 2005*

The aircraft carrier *Abraham Lincoln* was among the US Navy ships chosen to assist in the tsunami relief mission.

at Pearl Harbor in Honolulu, Hawaii, Admiral Thomas Fargo began planning a response. Indonesia was in dire need of disaster relief. Early figures suggested the tsunami had claimed the lives of approximately 10,000 people.[5] Over the next three days, the figure rose dramatically. PACOM drastically widened the scope of the mission, which it called Operation Unified Assistance. The US Department of Defense reported the purpose of the mission was to "prevent further loss of life and human suffering by expeditiously applying resources to the overall relief effort."[6]

PACOM established Joint Task Force 536 to carry out the mission. It was renamed Combined Support Force 536 when it became a multinational coalition including forces from Australia, Japan, Singapore, Russia, France, and Malaysia.

By December 28, naval ships arrived in Thailand to set up a command center. More ships arrived in Sri Lanka and Indonesia. The next day, P-3 Orion reconnaissance aircraft took off to assess damage in the region. Soon, other planes began dropping supplies. Working together with the US Army, Air Force, and Marines, the navy worked to get supplies, personnel, and medical attention to the disaster-ravaged areas of Southeast Asia.

THE *MERCY*

The *Mercy*, like its sister ship the *Comfort*, serves as a floating hospital offering medical support to soldiers, sailors, or civilian disaster victims. It has 12 operating rooms and can accommodate up to 1,000 patient beds.[7] During Operation Unified Assistance, approximately 275 medical and support personnel sailed with *Mercy*'s humanitarian mission. The ship was prepared to treat cases of infectious diseases, dehydration, and malnutrition in patients ranging from young children to the elderly. The ship is 894 feet (272.5 m) in length and has a top speed of approximately 20 miles per hour (32 kmh).[8] When ordered to activate, the ship must be stocked, prepared, and ready to sail within five days.

AID ON LAND AND AT SEA

The tsunami caused death and destruction in an arc from Sri Lanka and India to Indonesia. The navy's prime focus was on the island of Sumatra in northern Indonesia. The aircraft carrier *Abraham Lincoln,* accompanied by several other vessels, left Hong Kong for Indonesia, where it would meet up with a seven-ship force led by the amphibious assault ship *Bonhomme Richard.* On January 1, 2005, the US

Department of Defense activated the *Mercy,* a hospital ship stationed in San Diego, California. A few days later, the *Mercy* departed for Southeast Asia. Staffed with an expert medical team, it would provide a floating hospital for victims of the tsunami.

When the *Abraham Lincoln* arrived in Indonesia, the tsunami waves were long gone. Left behind were destruction and death. Garbage, debris, and bodies floated in the water. Navy staff hustled to set up temporary hospital facilities to treat the injured while others got to work producing clean, safe drinking water. Those who

US Navy helicopters carried critical supplies from aircraft carriers to places in need.

had survived the tsunami were now in peril of dying from dehydration, starvation, or disease. Navy personnel filled jugs with clean water and dropped them by helicopter, along with bags of rice and food, to Indonesians up and down the coast. The navy deployed 19 SH-60 Seahawk helicopters from the *Abraham Lincoln*'s carrier strike group to fly reconnaissance, evacuation, and relief missions over Indonesia.[9]

The *Tippecanoe, John Ericsson, San Jose,* and *Ranier* provided fuel and supplies to support other ships and personnel in the tsunami relief area. In mid-January, the research ships *Mary Sears* and *John McDonnell* were ordered into the affected area to conduct studies of the ocean floor where the earthquake had occurred. Each ship had its own job, and every sailor, officer, and medical team member had an individual responsibility.

Faced with the task of bringing comfort and hope to thousands of mourning people left without homes, the navy was ready. Personnel had trained for situations similar to this, and they knew how to work together to respond quickly and efficiently in the face of devastation.

A few weeks after the earthquake and tsunami, Operation Unified Assistance included more than 25 US Navy ships, 58 helicopters, and 45 airplanes. By January 5, the US military had delivered more than 610,000 pounds (280,000 kg) of water, food, and supplies to the region.[10]

The *Abraham Lincoln* remained in the area for a month as navy personnel continued assisting tsunami victims.

As a result of the combined relief efforts of the US Navy, Army, Air Force, and Marines, Indonesian public opinion of the United States improved remarkably. While one important purpose of the US military is to offer defense against foreign military forces, it often takes on missions to offer humanitarian assistance and relief. These missions not only enhance the international standing of the United States, but also provide a chance for the navy to practice its logistical skills. With its unmatched global reach, the US Navy stands at the ready to offer aid where and when it is needed.

AID IN THE PHILIPPINES

On November 8, 2013, Typhoon Haiyan struck the Philippines and other portions of Southeast Asia, killing more than 5,000 people.[11] It was the deadliest Philippine typhoon on record and one of the strongest storms ever to hit land. Haiyan devastated portions of the Philippines, particularly the city of Tacloban, which was estimated to be nearly 90 percent destroyed.[12] Some portions of the area were completely washed away. The US Navy was deployed to offer humanitarian aid to the area through Joint Task Force 505. The aircraft carrier *George Washington*, along with the other ships in its carrier strike group, was deployed to assist with Operation Damayan in the Philippines.

CHAPTER TWO

A NAVY FOR A NEW COUNTRY

The US Navy is relatively new when compared to the navies of such countries as the United Kingdom, Spain, Portugal, and China. It traces its roots to the Continental navy, which fought for independence from Great Britain during the American Revolutionary War (1775–1783).

Though the Continental navy was dramatically overmatched against Great Britain, it won several key victories.

While humble in its beginnings, the first vessels of this ancestor of the US Navy proved to be effective in battle.

The American colonies had a rich tradition of seafaring. A large community of fishermen, sailors, and shipbuilders lived along the East Coast and were familiar with ships and sailing. In 1775, when the colonies declared

A NAVAL HERO

John Paul Jones, a Scottish merchant shipmaster, sailed to America in 1775 and volunteered to serve on the American side during the Revolutionary War. He was made a lieutenant and later a captain, and he is remembered as an outstanding officer. During a battle with the British vessel *Serapis*, Jones's damaged flagship *Bonhomme Richard* and his small squadron fought one of the bloodiest battles in US naval history. With the *Bonhomme Richard* burning and sinking, the British demanded Jones's surrender. Jones replied with his famous line, "I have not yet begun to fight!"[2] More than three hours later, following a dramatic battle, Jones accepted the surrender of the *Serapis* and took command of the British ship. John Paul Jones has become a naval legend and the most famous sailor from the Revolutionary War era.

their independence from Great Britain and went to war, two privately owned American ships intercepted guns and supplies transported on British vessels. On October 13, the Continental Congress authorized the two vessels to cruise in search of munitions ships supplying the British army. This act is considered to be the birth of the Continental navy.

THE CONTINENTAL NAVY

The first navy warships were simply merchant ships converted for combat by adding guns and large sails that would make them faster. The Continental navy consisted of approximately 60 vessels large and strong enough to challenge British warships.[1] In addition, 11 of the colonies had their own navies, aiding the war effort on the water. Privately owned ships also contributed to the struggle.

Throughout the war, the Continental navy and privateers captured enemy war goods and gave them to the army, transported diplomats to foreign countries, raided British shipping routes, and put up a brave defense of American coastal waters. By the war's end, most of the ships had been sunk. Only a few still sailed. With domestic matters seeming more important than maintaining a postwar naval force, the remaining vessels were sold and the Continental navy was disbanded in 1785.

PRIVATEERS

Privateers were private citizens who owned ships and were authorized by the government to attack foreign vessels in times of war. To authorize them, the government gave them a paper called a letter of marque. This practice reduced the amount of money a country would have to spend on its navy. Privateers received a portion of the value of the captured vessels and their cargo. However, if the enemy's navy captured privateers, they would become prisoners of war.

THE REBIRTH OF THE NAVY

Not long after the war with Britain ended, the young United States discovered a need for a naval fleet once again. French sea raiders off the coast of North Africa, also known as corsairs, were attacking US merchant ships and capturing and killing sailors.

In 1794, the US Congress decided to protect the nation's merchant ships in international waters by building a strong navy. Construction began on six frigates, but progress was slow. By 1798, conditions became so desperate that Congress sped up the ships' completion to get the new navy into action right away. France and Britain were at war, and by 1798 French forces had seized more than 300 US merchant ships, causing relations between France and the United States to reach a tense state of undeclared war. The United States launched the *Constitution* and *United States*, both 44-gun frigates,

The *Constitution* is still a part of the US Navy today. It is the oldest working warship in the world.

along with the *Constellation,* a 36-gun frigate, to lead the new fleet.

The government purchased 12 more ships and created a new agency to oversee operations. The Department of the Navy was born on April 30, 1798. Benjamin Stoddert of Maryland became the first secretary of the navy. In his first year in office, he ordered the construction of 49 ships. The new navy's victories mounted. By the end of 1799, the expert seamanship of US officers had led to the capture of dozens of French ships. The next year, the frigate *Essex* sailed around the Horn of Africa and through the Indian Ocean, recapturing many seized US ships and driving away numerous French vessels.

President John Adams responded to these victories by stating, "The present Navy of the United States, called suddenly into existence by a great national emergency, has raised us in our own esteem."[3] The undeclared war with France came to an end in 1800, one year after Napoleón I came to power in France.

THE BARBARY WARS

By 1801, the situation for US merchant ships off the coast of North Africa had once again become hostile. Pirates from Tripoli, one of the Barbary States, resumed seizing US ships after President Thomas Jefferson refused to pay large sums of money.

The burning of the *Philadelphia* has become one of the most famous incidents in the early history of the US Navy.

On May 20, 1801, the secretary of the navy dispatched the frigates *President*, *Philadelphia*, and *Essex*, as well as the schooner *Enterprise*, to the Mediterranean Sea. The battles that ensued became known as the First Barbary War (1801–1805). During the war, the *Philadelphia* was captured and its men taken prisoner. In a valiant effort to thwart the use of the seized ship, US Navy Lieutenant Stephen Decatur of the *Essex* led a small group of US troops on a mission to stealthily approach the ship, board it, and set it on fire. The group succeeded in their mission. Decatur became a national hero.

THE WAR OF 1812

Less than 40 years after the humble Continental navy put up a brave fight against experienced British warships, the US again found itself at war with Great Britain, by this time known as the United Kingdom. The strength of the growing US Navy would be put to the test.

The United Kingdom had gone to war with France in 1803. At that time, the United Kingdom declared a blockade of France, using its vast fleet to block shipments from reaching French shores. The United Kingdom proceeded to seize US merchant ships that violated the blockade. Hundreds of US sailors were forced into service for the United Kingdom's Royal Navy. Among other grievances, this issue led the United States to declare

THE *CHESAPEAKE-LEOPARD* AFFAIR

In the early 1800s, British captains became so brazen they would station their frigates just off the East Coast of the United States and seize sailors while still in view of US ports. Any man who could not provide proof of being born in the United States was forced into service, regardless of where they were born. This act was known as impressment. Many of those taken were US immigrants originally from Ireland. In 1807, the US ship *Chesapeake* was stopped just outside of Norfolk, Virginia, by the British ship *Leopard*. The Royal Navy demanded Captain James Barron give up any British citizens. When Barron refused, the *Leopard* opened fire on the *Chesapeake,* severely damaging the ship. Barron lowered his flag and gave up the men. Americans were outraged and the country was brought one step closer to war.

The *Constitution*'s destruction of the *Guerriere* has been commemorated in several paintings.

war against the United Kingdom on June 18, 1812. The conflict became known as the War of 1812 (1812–1815).

At the time, the United States had only 16 warships.[4] The Royal Navy had approximately 1,000 warships.[5] Yet, because the Royal Navy was preoccupied with war against France, the US Navy experienced several brilliant victories. The *Constitution* destroyed the *Guerriere* and the *Java,* and the *United States* captured the *Macedonian.*

The Royal Navy blockaded US ports, but private vessels continued to operate, assisting the US Navy by capturing hundreds of enemy ships. The US Navy was victorious in 11 single-ship duels against the Royal

Navy, and its defeat of British squadrons on Lake Erie and Lake Champlain helped ensure the United States would not have to give up land to the British after the war's end in 1815. The US Navy had successfully defended its homeland in time of war.

IMPRESSING THE WORLD

The power of the young US Navy far outclassed any expectations people had about it. Edgar Stanton Maclay, author in 1894 of *A History of the United States Navy, from 1775 to 1893*, noted:

> At the outbreak of the War of 1812 the British navy was in the zenith of its glory. It had matched its strength against the combined navies of the greatest maritime nations of the world, and had come off a victor. But in two and a half years of naval war with the United States British commerce was almost annihilated, and in eighteen naval engagements the Royal Navy sustained fifteen defeats; and this after the London Statesman of June 10, 1812 had said, "America certainly can not pretend to wage war with us; she has no navy to do it with."[6]

CHAPTER THREE
A NAVAL POWERHOUSE

I n 1845, the US Navy opened a new school in Annapolis, Maryland. The US Naval School began training future officers. Secretary of the Navy George Bancroft established the school on the site of a former US Army post, Fort Severn. By 1851, the school was reorganized

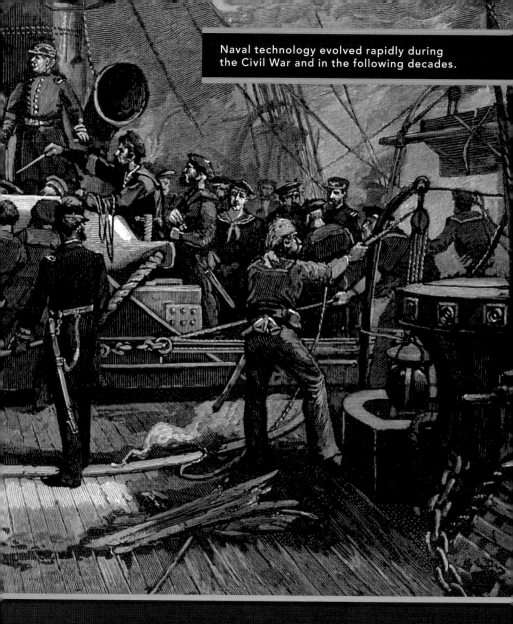
Naval technology evolved rapidly during the Civil War and in the following decades.

and took on the name it maintains to the present: the US Naval Academy.

When the American Civil War (1861–1865) erupted, the long land border between the two sides suggested the US Navy might not play an important role in the conflict. Additionally, there was a wide divide between the sides'

THE US NAVAL ACADEMY

Since 1845, the US Naval Academy in Annapolis, Maryland, has been training young midshipmen to become officers in the US Navy and Marine Corps. Candidates applying for admission typically must receive a nomination from a congressperson, a senator, the vice president, or the president. Alternatively, candidates can be the son or daughter of a recipient of the Medal of Honor, the highest military award. Applicants must also achieve high scores on standardized tests. The academy admits approximately 7 percent of those who apply.[3]

navies. The northern states, forming the Union, possessed more ships than the southern states, known as the Confederacy. However, the improvised naval forces of the Confederacy would test the Union navy. In the end, the advances made by the US Navy during the war transformed it into a world leader in naval activity. It entered the Civil War with 42 ships. Four years later, it possessed 670 of them.[1]

THE CIVIL WAR

During the Civil War, the US Navy set up a blockade of the 3,500-mile (5,600 km) southern coastline.[2] Although the ships were spread thin to blockade the coast, the Union navy was effective in disrupting exports of cotton and imports of war supplies. This hastened the eventual collapse of the Confederacy. The navy gained valuable offensive experience in long-range weapons and troop landings when it captured ports and the forts protecting them, such as North Carolina's Fort Fisher.

Additionally, the US Navy engaged in extensive river warfare. Admirals David Farragut, Andrew Foote, and David D. Porter attacked Confederate forts along the Mississippi River and its major tributaries. They used imaginative watercraft, such as armored boats and vessels with metal rams below the water that slashed the bottoms of Confederate ships. The engineers of the Confederacy employed their own ingenuity by crafting ships protected with bales of cotton and by using naval mines. These underwater explosive devices sank dozens of Union ships.

One of the most famous naval encounters of the Civil War involved the Union's *Monitor* and the Confederacy's *Virginia*. In the Battle of Hampton Roads, off the coast of Virginia, the vessels engaged in the first direct struggle between two heavily armored ships, known as ironclads. The ships exchanged cannon fire, each withstanding an incredible number of hits. The result was a draw, but the impact of this demonstration on later naval

THE *MONITOR* AND THE *VIRGINIA*

The South sent the *Virginia* up against a fleet of wooden Union ships. Because metal plating protected the *Virginia*, the ship was thought to be indestructible. It sank the *Cumberland* and burned the *Congress* on March 8, 1862. The following day, the Confederates were surprised to see a Union vessel with similar armor. The *Monitor* had arrived to challenge the *Virginia*. The two heavy, awkward ships exchanged fire for several hours. Finally, the *Virginia* withdrew from the battle. The age of armored warships had begun.

The *Virginia, left,* and the *Monitor, right,* helped bring an end to the era of wooden ships.

vessels was enormous. Armored ships, considered a novelty only a few years before, soon became vital parts of the world's fleets. When the Civil War finally ended in 1865, the United States had the world's most powerful navy.

THE SPANISH-AMERICAN WAR

When the Civil War drew to a close, the US Navy was cut back. Ships were sold and scrapped for economic and strategic reasons, and the navy returned to using sails instead of steam engines. Nevertheless, the officers and sailors who came out of the Civil War had gained knowledge and discipline, and naval forces had made great strides in technology and tactics. In the 1880s, the US government began modernizing its fleet once again. The navy switched to building future ships from steel instead of wood.

In 1896, relations between Spain and Cuba became tense. To help protect US citizens in Cuba, President William McKinley sent the battleship *Maine* to Havana, Cuba's capital. Three weeks later, on February 15, 1898, the ship exploded, killing 260 sailors and officers. The true cause of the explosion remains a mystery, but blame fell on Spain. Congress declared war, bringing the nation into the Spanish-American War (1898). The struggle involved battles over Spanish possessions in the Atlantic and Pacific Oceans. Seeking justice for the loss of the men of the *Maine*, the navy set out with a strong resolve and won two important victories. Commodore George Dewey and his squadron steamed into Manila Bay in the Philippines in the early morning of May 1 and destroyed or captured a fleet of nine Spanish ships anchored there.

In the Atlantic Ocean, Commodore William T. Sampson led a squadron in pursuit of Spanish vessels. The US battleships *Oregon*, *Texas*, *Iowa*, and *Indiana* led a chase that ended in the destruction of Spanish forces outside

Eugene Ely's takeoff from the *Birmingham* represented the birth of US naval aviation.

Santiago, Cuba. Spain lost more than 300 men; a further 1,800 were captured. The United States lost one man, and another was wounded.[4] As part of Spain's surrender, the country ceded Puerto Rico, Guam, and the Philippines to the United States.

A TWENTIETH-CENTURY NAVY

As the new century dawned, major changes began developing in the US Navy. In 1911, the navy purchased its first airplane. Naval aviation was born, and by 1914, the country's first permanent naval air station was established at Pensacola, Florida. Decades before US aircraft were brought under the command of a separate branch, the air force, the navy and the army had their own airplanes. At this point, the navy's aircraft were mostly floatplanes, designed to take off and land directly on the water.

The United States entered World War I (1914–1918) on April 6, 1917. The Central powers, including Germany and Austria-Hungary, faced off against the Allies, including the United Kingdom and later the United States. A key challenge for the US Navy was countering German submarine warfare. German submarines had ravaged British shipping. Without assistance, the United Kingdom would face dangerous shortages of supplies. The United States answered by sending convoys of US ships with cargo and troops. Naval ships, merchant ships, and aircraft offered protection against German submarines for the convoys on the way to Europe.

FROM OCEAN TO AIR

Prior to 1910, the thought of an airplane taking off or landing on a ship seemed ridiculous. It had only been seven years since the Wright brothers flew the world's first successful piloted airplane. But on November 14, 1910, pilot Eugene Ely performed the first shipboard takeoff from the US cruiser *Birmingham*. Two months later, on January 18, 1911, Ely demonstrated a landing on the *Pennsylvania*, a battleship docked in San Francisco, California. He then took off from the deck of the *Pennsylvania* and returned to shore. Ely's daring feats significantly altered the future of maritime power. Ely soon joined Glenn H. Curtiss in experimenting with dropping makeshift bombs on floating targets in lakes. Curtiss realized "the battles of the future will be fought in the air."[5]

After the war, the US Navy entered a period of decline. One key postwar addition to the navy was the 1922 commissioning of the *Langley*, the nation's first aircraft carrier. Launching and landing planes from aircraft carriers would make it possible for the United States to project its power overseas. The capability would prove critically important in the coming decades. In 1936, recognizing a potential impending war, President Franklin D. Roosevelt launched a program to strengthen the navy. Shipbuilding resumed and included the construction of battleships, submarines, and aircraft carriers. The decision would prove to be a wise one, as the world was indeed inching closer to war.

The *Langley* was the first step in a series of technological developments that eventually led to the nuclear aircraft carriers of today.

WORLD WAR II

On December 7, 1941, Japan attacked the US naval base
at Pearl Harbor on the Hawaiian island of Oahu. Fighter
planes and bombers from distant aircraft carriers flew
in undetected and destroyed airfields and aircraft on the
ground before continuing on to bomb the fleet of ships
in the harbor. The ships sunk included the battleship
Arizona, the destroyers *Cassin*, *Downes*, and *Shaw*, and the
minelayer *Oglala*. By the end of the devastating surprise
attack, 2,388 Americans had been killed, including 48
civilians.[6] Another 1,178 people were wounded.[7] The US
Navy's Pacific fleet was crippled. As Americans listened
to radio reports in shocked horror, a swell of patriotism
swept the nation. The country pulled together to carry out
revenge, and Congress declared war on Japan. The United
States entered World War II (1939–1945) one day after the
Pearl Harbor attack. The Axis powers, including Germany
and Japan, fought the Allies, including the United States,
United Kingdom, and the Soviet Union.

As in the Spanish-American War, the US Navy fought
in both the Atlantic and Pacific Oceans. Admiral Chester
W. Nimitz commanded the Pacific Fleet, and Admiral
Royal E. Ingersoll commanded the Atlantic Fleet. The navy
built and launched thousands of new ships during World
War II. The fleets commanded by Admiral Nimitz won
several victories in the Pacific theater, ending Japanese

expansion. In one of the most important battles, the Battle of Midway, US intelligence services took advantage of a broken Japanese code to predict a planned attack. When the Japanese forces arrived in early June 1942, US carriers and warships were waiting. In a battle fought almost entirely by carrier-based planes, US forces sank four Japanese aircraft carriers and several other ships. The United States claimed a major victory, marking the turning point in the Pacific War.

In the Atlantic Ocean, the navies of the United States and its allies faced German submarines, which sank thousands of ships. The Allies eventually overcame the threat by utilizing sonar systems, patrolling aircraft, and intercepted German radio messages to find enemy vessels. Ships used sinking bombs called depth charges to destroy submarines.

WOMEN ENTER THE NAVY

Women first served in the US Navy during World War I. In order to make more men available for service on ships, women worked in clerical and secretarial positions. Later, during World War II, Congress authorized the Women's Reserve, a special branch of the Navy Reserve. The branch was officially called Women Accepted for Volunteer Emergency Service, or WAVES. Members took part in many fields, including aviation, communications, research, and intelligence. Six years later, in 1948, women were permanently accepted into some positions as part of the regular US Navy and the Navy Reserve. With the exception of some special forces positions, women can now hold any job in the US Navy.

The US battleships of World War II, including the *Iowa*, could bring incredible firepower to the battlefield. The ship is shown here in 1984.

The navy achieved a spectacular victory when it successfully transported millions of Allied troops to German-occupied Europe during the invasion of France. Navy ships pounded German coastal defenses with long-range guns, preparing the beaches for US Navy and Coast Guard landing boats. Army troops rushed off the boats into the heated battle. Though the Allies sustained heavy losses, they successfully took a foothold in Western Europe. By the end of World War II, the United States possessed the world's largest and most powerful navy by a wide margin.

THE KOREAN WAR AND THE VIETNAM WAR

Five years after the war, the United States returned to the battlefield in the Korean War (1950–1953). Aircraft carriers, troop transports, and amphibious landing craft helped reverse the course of the war. Despite a spectacularly successful naval invasion at the Battle of Inchon, the war eventually ended in a stalemate. The line dividing North Korea and South Korea remains in place to this day.

In the 1950s, the US Navy set to work building faster and more powerful aircraft and ships. Aircraft carriers and submarines were equipped with nuclear power, allowing them to operate for months or even years without refueling.

The United States next became involved in the Vietnam War (1955–1975). The war pitted Communist North Vietnam against US-backed South Vietnam. Fighters sympathetic to North Vietnam lay in hiding throughout South Vietnam. Starting in 1964, the US Navy was tasked with patrolling the rivers and coastline of South Vietnam. Air strikes launched from aircraft carriers, along with cruisers, destroyers, and battleships on the sea, bombarded enemy forces throughout Vietnam. Despite the efforts of the navy and the rest of the US military, victory in Vietnam proved elusive. The United States withdrew its military in 1973, and North Vietnam overran South Vietnam in 1975.

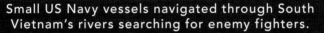
Small US Navy vessels navigated through South Vietnam's rivers searching for enemy fighters.

THE US NAVY IN THE MIDDLE EAST

The United States entered the Persian Gulf War (1991) when war broke out between Iraq and several other nations following Iraq's invasion of Kuwait. US Navy aircraft struck Iraqi armored units and military installations while battleships hit Iraqi targets from the water.

During the Iraq War (2003–2011), US Navy aircraft carriers provided fighters and helicopters. Special forces, including Navy SEALs, were deployed for reconnaissance missions and small unit attacks. During the War on Terror (2001–), SEALs have been tasked with searching for high-ranking terrorist leaders, such as Osama bin Laden.

Aerial refueling from large tanker aircraft enabled US Navy fighter jets to carry out long-duration missions during the Persian Gulf War.

CHAPTER FOUR
THE ROLE OF THE US NAVY

The stated mission of the US Navy is to "maintain, train, and equip combat-ready naval forces capable of winning wars, deterring aggression, and maintaining freedom of the seas."[1] In order to fulfill this mission, the navy maintains a force of more than 300,000 active-duty service members.[2] An additional 71,000 people serve in

the Navy Reserve and are ready to be called to active duty
on short notice.[3]

    The US Navy maintains a surface fleet, a submarine
fleet, a naval aviation wing, and support forces on land.
The surface fleet consists of vessels of all shapes and sizes.
From the largest aircraft carrier on the open ocean to the

smallest boats maneuvering through narrow rivers, the navy's surface fleet is equipped to carry out any mission on the water. Under the water, the submarine fleet carries out missions in both wartime and peacetime. Submarines play a vital role in attack, surveillance, and research. They also help quietly deliver elite combat troops, known as special forces, where they need to go. Some submarines carry missiles armed with nuclear weapons. Alongside bomber aircraft and land-based missiles, they represent one-third of the United States' nuclear force.

The naval aviation wing consists of helicopters, surveillance planes, transport and cargo aircraft, fighter

The navy is known for its fleet of ships and aircraft, but its members also train for important land-based functions.

and attack jets, and unmanned aerial vehicles commonly known as drones. Land-based support forces provide repairs, training, communications, intelligence, and weather information, among other tasks.

AROUND THE WORLD

The United States has ships and personnel to support both a blue-water navy and a brown-water navy. The name *blue-water navy* describes naval forces that can operate far from the coast. A *brown-water navy* consists of ships that remain in inland waters and near the coast. The United States now often uses *green-water navy* to describe the portion of the fleet that defends coasts, reserving *brown-water navy* for river forces.

The US Navy operates from many naval bases around the world. Bases are ports and airfields designed to support and supply the navy by providing housing, docks, munitions depots, aviation support, and repair facilities. Some naval bases provide training as well. The United States maintains naval bases, also called installations, in coastal countries around the world. The United States has naval installations in more than 15 countries, including Egypt, Cuba, Greece, Italy, Japan, Kuwait, Singapore, and Spain.[4] Additionally, the United States has naval facilities in more than 25 states.[5]

WARTIME RESPONSIBILITIES

During times of war, the US Navy defends the United States against enemies at sea, on land, and in the air. Fleets work together to attack with torpedoes, missiles, naval artillery, and other weapons. Other tools at the navy's disposal include warships, fighter jets, and helicopters.

The navy also provides transportation for US Marines and Army troops using ships, airplanes, and helicopters. Jobs range from transporting one person, such as a key admiral or general, to moving a large group of personnel overseas.

HUMANITARIAN RELIEF

The US Navy has a long history of assisting with disaster relief. The navy has experience bringing comfort and hope to victims of natural disasters such as hurricanes and tsunamis. Navy personnel are trained to work together

INSTALLATIONS AROUND THE WORLD

Naval installations can be found in many locations around the globe. From Bahrain to Brazil, Greece to Guam, and many places in between, the US Navy has bases abroad that serve as training centers, research facilities, and homes to ships and aircraft. Guantanamo Bay in Cuba is the United States' oldest overseas naval base.

The base has been in operation since 1903, when the Cuban-American Treaty permitted the United States to lease Guantanamo Bay. Usually, countries with US military bases have good relations with the United States. Cuba, however, has been protesting against the US Navy presence in Guantanamo Bay since 1959.

US NAVY INSTALLATIONS

swiftly and efficiently to deliver basic needs such as food, drinkable water, and shelter. Engineers and technicians set up water purification systems, clear debris, and establish safe areas for shelter construction. Forces in helicopters deliver emergency supplies to disaster victims and conduct rescue missions to assist stranded or injured people. The navy also possesses two floating hospital ships. The *Mercy* and the *Comfort* can be deployed to areas of disaster to offer medical care to victims and their families.

In addition to disaster relief, the US Navy also participates in other humanitarian efforts. One such project is Operation Smile, a worldwide children's medical charity that provides surgery for children in developing countries who are born with facial deformities. As part of the program, the US Navy offers the services of naval doctors and dentists to people who otherwise would not receive this type of medical attention. These medical missions bring together international staffs of medical personnel who provide surgeries, help build hospitals, and educate people in developing countries about health. The humanitarian efforts of the US Navy have helped to improve the public opinion of the United States around the world.

TIME FOR A NEW SLOGAN?

Although the US Navy does not have an official motto, in 2009 it rolled out a new recruiting campaign with the slogan "America's Navy: A Global Force for Good." While the "force for good" slogan may have aimed at calling attention to the humanitarian efforts of the navy, not everyone was pleased with the new ads. A poll of service members and veterans reported a strong dislike for the "global force" slogan, as they believed it did not accurately represent the day-to-day life of sailors. Further polls of the general public showed that 70 percent of people believe the navy's mission is to protect and defend the United States, not serve as a global force for good.[6]

The *Mercy* and the *Comfort* are equipped with high-quality operating facilities.

INTERNATIONAL COOPERATION

The US Navy cooperates with navies around the world to protect against the increasingly serious problem of piracy. In the ongoing war against pirates threatening merchant vessels in international waters, the navy has partnered with 26 nations in creating a combined maritime force.

The mission of this partnership is to promote security, stability, and prosperity across international waters in the Middle East and Southeast Asia. These 2.5 million square

A US Navy officer explains equipment on the *Samuel Roberts* to an officer from the navy of the African nation of Djibouti.

miles (6.5 million sq km) of water comprise some of the world's most important shipping routes. Thanks in part to this cooperative effort, reports of vessels attacked by pirates decreased from 45 in 2009 to 22 in 2011.[7]

TECHNOLOGICAL ADVANCES AND CONTRIBUTIONS

The US Navy has provided the world with numerous advances in technology. It has spearheaded the evolution of maritime vessels from wooden sailing ships to nuclear-powered steel vessels. Carrier-based aviation was also a product of the navy. The first airplanes used for aerial reconnaissance at sea were the forerunners of today's high-tech fighter and attack jets.

The world's first attempted submarine attack took place during the American Revolutionary War when a US vessel tried to attach a mine to a British warship. The navy improved submarine warfare throughout the decades and perfected the use of torpedoes. Later, guided missiles were designed to attack distant enemy ships with an increasing degree of accuracy.

THE US NAVAL RESEARCH LABORATORY

For the past 90 years, the Naval Research Laboratory (NRL) has served the nation through scientific research. It is the research lab for the US Navy and Marine Corps. Scientists and engineers at the NRL have won many prestigious awards. Two shared the 1985 Nobel Prize for Chemistry. The laboratory, headquartered in Washington, DC, was responsible for developing shipboard radar and is a leader in research on electronic warfare and artificial intelligence.

CHAPTER FIVE
VESSELS OF THE US NAVY

Naval ships perform many functions. Some serve as portable, floating landing strips for airplanes. Others transport supplies and goods. Some carry ground crews and specialized equipment, while others protect aircraft carriers or attack enemy ships. Working together, US naval

ships defend the United States and support the US military at sea.

The US Navy operates approximately 280 ships and more than 3,700 aircraft.[1] Today it is the world's largest navy by a wide margin. Naval vessels can be divided into two categories, combat ships and auxiliary ships. Combat

THE GREAT WHITE FLEET

In 1907, President Theodore Roosevelt sought to display the power of the US Navy's new battleships. Sixteen battleships were painted white and sent on a 14-month world tour. The Great White Fleet visited 20 ports on six continents. Departing from Virginia, they traveled south around the Americas and back up to California before sailing across the Pacific Ocean to Hawaii, Japan, and Australia. The ships next went to Egypt and passed through the Suez Canal into the Mediterranean Sea. From there, they visited Italy, sailed back into the Atlantic Ocean, and returned to Virginia.

ships participate in battle, while auxiliary ships provide services such as maintenance, refueling, supply, and towing. Combat ships include aircraft carriers, cruisers, destroyers, frigates, amphibious warships, and submarines.

During World War II, aircraft carriers began to overtake battleships as the key vessels in the fleet. Naval strategy planners later decided that naval aviation and advanced missile technology have made large battleships obsolete. Battleships no longer serve in the US Navy.

AIRCRAFT CARRIERS

Nicknamed "flattops" because of their wide, flat decks, aircraft carriers are the largest ships in the navy. They are used as mobile bases for aircraft, including fighter planes and helicopters, which are able to take off and land on the ship's top, called the flight deck. Powerful catapults help planes reach takeoff speed quickly. When landing, hooks on the aircraft grab cables on the flight deck, bringing planes to a swift stop.

The US Navy currently has ten aircraft carriers, each belonging to the Nimitz class, named for the commander of the Pacific fleet during World War II. The first entered service in 1975. Nimitz-class carriers measure 1,092 feet (333 m) in length and are 252 feet (77 m) wide at the flight deck.[2] They are capable of carrying 85 aircraft and approximately 5,700 crew members.[3]

The hangar deck, just below the flight deck, serves as a storage and repair area for aircraft. The ship's superstructure rises on the flight deck's starboard side and serves as the command and navigation center. It is home to communications equipment and radar antennae.

An aircraft carrier also has maintenance shops for the aircraft, living quarters for crew, cooking and eating areas, and storage for fuel, food, ammunition, and bombs. Nimitz-class carriers are nuclear powered and can operate for more than 20 years before needing to be refueled. They are designed for 50 years of service.

While aircraft carriers are the largest warships in the world, they do not travel alone. Cruisers, destroyers, and submarines travel with aircraft carriers to protect them from enemy ships, planes, and missiles. Together, the carrier and its associated ships are called a carrier task force. Using its ships and planes, a carrier task force can attack targets on land, in the sea, and in the air.

Constructing a modern aircraft carrier, such as the *Gerald R. Ford*, is an enormous and complex endeavor.

The first next-generation aircraft carrier, belonging to the Gerald R. Ford class, was under construction in 2014 and scheduled to enter service in 2016. The new carriers are designed to be more efficient, requiring fewer crew members. Electric catapults, allowing for more precise launches, have replaced steam-powered aircraft catapults. Additionally, the carriers' superstructures are positioned further back on the ship, allowing for a flight deck with more surface area. The estimated cost of the first ship, the *Gerald R. Ford*, was approximately $8.5 billion.[4]

CRUISERS, DESTROYERS, AND FRIGATES

The main task of guided missile cruisers is to escort aircraft carriers and support amphibious ships, those that deliver ground troops to shore. Cruisers are medium-sized warships that conduct antiaircraft, antimissile, and antisubmarine warfare. They can work alone or as a member of a larger group of ships. They are fast-moving ships capable of launching long-range missiles, allowing them to strike land or sea targets. They are also armed with powerful guns and torpedoes. Most US cruisers are named for famous battles in US military history.

Destroyers are surface ships that defend aircraft carriers and other ships using missiles and helicopters that can operate from their decks. These medium-sized vessels are deployed as part of task forces. Destroyers in the US Navy are named after important navy personnel and heroes. The latest type of destroyers, the

NAMING THE SHIPS

When new navy ships are constructed, they must be named. The secretary of the navy is responsible for selecting names, but others help with the task. Research is done to gather a list of possible names based upon navy history. Additionally, retired and active-duty sailors contribute ideas and suggestions to the list. Sometimes, members of the general public even suggest names for new ships.

Zumwalt class, was introduced in 2013. These ships look far different from the destroyers that came before. Their sleek profiles and quiet engines are designed to hide from enemy radar, and their automated systems are designed to require fewer crew members to operate.

Frigates also help escort aircraft carriers and other warships. They defend against submarine attacks through use of torpedoes and helicopters. Frigates also provide protection to supply convoys as well as merchant ships. In times of peace, frigates are also put to work intercepting illegal drug shipments and disrupting other illegal activity on the ocean. Like destroyers, these vessels are named

The Zumwalt-class destroyers feature a radical new design.

for naval heroes. However, frigates are smaller and carry fewer crew.

AMPHIBIOUS WARSHIPS

The navy's amphibious warships are designed to carry out and support invasions from the sea. The largest of these are amphibious assault ships, which look like small aircraft carriers. These vessels feature a flight deck for helicopters and small aircraft. Amphibious assault ships also feature a well deck, an area near the waterline that can be flooded to launch smaller amphibious ships for beach landings. They are armed with missiles and machine guns, but the ships' primary purpose is to transport troops and equipment near a coast so they can be offloaded using aircraft and landing vessels.

The actual beach landing is done by Landing Craft, Air Cushioned (LCAC) and Landing Craft, Mechanized and Utility (LCM/LCU). LCACs are large hovercraft that ride on a layer of air generated by enormous fans rather than directly on the ocean's surface. This gives the vessels a high speed and also permits them to land in more areas than traditional landing craft. LCM/LCUs are smaller vehicles with ramps to offload supplies and soldiers onto beaches.

SUBMARINES

Submarines protect the carrier task force below the ocean's surface. They are able to quietly approach enemy ships and attack them underwater. Submarines also engage in surveillance and intelligence missions. Some submarines carry and launch missiles at targets on land. Others sink ships and other submarines using torpedoes. Submarines that fire nuclear missiles are called ballistic missile submarines. Those that fire torpedoes are called attack submarines.

THE NAVY GOES NUCLEAR

In 1955, the US Navy launched its first nuclear-powered submarine, the *Nautilus*. Since that time, many nuclear-powered vessels have been built. The *Enterprise* became the first nuclear-powered aircraft carrier in 1961. Today, all US carriers are nuclear powered. Nuclear reactors onboard the ships provide power, making refueling unnecessary for several years.

The US Navy's newest class of attack submarines is the Virginia class. Production of these nuclear-powered vessels began in 2000. Each 377-foot (115 m) submarine costs approximately $2.7 billion.[5] Virginia-class submarines carry crews of 134 people. Information about their speed is classified, but experts estimate they can reach speeds of more than 29 miles per hour (47 kmh) on the surface and 37 miles per hour (60 kmh) when

The navy plans to continue building sleek Virginia-class submarines, such as the *California*, into the 2040s.

submerged underwater.[6] For their size and weight, the vessels are very fast.

AUXILIARY SHIPS

Naval auxiliary ships have the important job of supporting combat ships. They provide fuel, supplies, maintenance, and towing to other ships. Underway replenishment ships bring supplies to ships already at sea. These vessels transfer cargo to moving ships through the use of special lines rigged between the two ships.

Fleet support ships are called in when a combat ship needs maintenance or service. Their crews perform such tasks as towing, salvage, diving, heavy lifting, and firefighting. Special fleet support ships are designed to assist submarines. Hospital ships and tugboats are two other types of fleet support ships.

NAVAL AVIATION

The strength of the US Navy comes from more than just its ships and submarines. In addition to guns, torpedoes, missiles, and other weapons, the navy has a large fleet of aircraft. These aircraft are used to defend fleets, strike enemy ships and targets on shore, perform patrols, and assist with humanitarian efforts.

The F/A-18 Hornet and its advanced version, the Super Hornet, are multirole combat jets designed to accomplish a variety of missions. They use missiles and machine guns to attack enemy aircraft. They can launch antiship missiles to destroy enemy ships. Hornets and Super Hornets can also drop bombs on ground targets. The jets can travel at nearly twice the speed of sound and are agile in the sky. The Hornet entered service in 1980. It was later refined and upgraded into the Super Hornet, introduced in 1999. The Super Hornet is larger and can carry more fuel, giving it a longer range. The Hornet can fight in an approximately 330-mile (540 km) radius around its aircraft carrier, and the Super Hornet expands this to approximately 450 miles (720 km).[7]

Both the Hornet and the Super Hornet were specifically designed for use on aircraft carriers. Their wings fold up to occupy less space on the flight deck. They are built ruggedly to withstand the stress of catapult takeoffs and carrier landings.

In 2013, the US Navy began receiving its replacement for the Hornets, the F-35 Lightning II. The jet has three

Super Hornets make it possible for the navy to extend its power far inland.

variants. The first, for use by the air force, is the F-35A. It can land and take off on normal runways. The second, for use by the marines, is the F-35B. It is capable of landing on and taking off from short, rugged runways. The navy will use the third version, the F-35C. It can land and take off on aircraft carriers.

The fighter jets may be the flashiest aircraft in the navy arsenal, but other aircraft are also critical to the service's missions. The S-3B Viking is a jet aircraft used for surveillance. It is also able to battle enemy surface ships. The EA-6B Prowler is a jet aircraft equipped with special electronic equipment that jams enemy radar systems. This plane is crewed by one pilot and two or three electronic countermeasures officers.

The P-3 Orion has been used since the 1960s as an antisubmarine patrol aircraft. It is also a valuable tool for surveillance at sea or over land. The Orion was an important asset during the Iraq War. The aircraft's long range allowed pilots to view the battlefield from above and immediately report down to troops on the ground. The Orion uses special equipment to detect submarines even when they are submerged.

In addition to airplanes, the US Navy utilizes helicopters for attacking ships and submarines, conducting search and rescue operations, delivering supplies, and carrying out humanitarian missions. Some navy

Ship-launched missiles provide much greater range and accuracy than the cannons and naval guns of the past.

helicopters have even been called upon to help fight forest fires. The SH-60 Seahawk helicopter is based on aircraft carriers, destroyers, and frigates. It has special sensors to detect submarines and can be equipped with machine guns, torpedoes, and missiles. Often the Seahawk is called upon to deliver supplies and people from one ship to another.

The US Navy has a host of different weapons at its disposal. Bombs, guns, missiles, torpedoes, and mines are used to defend ships and aircraft and attack the enemy.

MK 45 guns mounted on cruisers and destroyers can hit targets more than ten miles (16 km) away. MK 75 rapid-fire guns are used on surface warships and can hit targets within a range of approximately 11.5 miles (18.5 km).[8]

The navy's antisubmarine missile system is capable of being used in a wide range of sea and weather conditions. It is used primarily on cruisers, destroyers, and frigates. The navy also uses several types of torpedoes to sink enemy ships. They can be air launched, surface launched, and subsurface launched.

The navy has a variety of missiles, including surface-to-air, air-to-air, air-to-surface, and mixed-use missiles that can hit ground targets from the surface or air. Ballistic missile submarines use Trident missiles to launch nuclear bombs. These missiles have a range of approximately 4,600 miles (7,400 km).[9] Tridents are launched from below the ocean's surface.

The Tomahawk cruise missile was first used in 1991 during the Persian Gulf War. It can be launched from either a surface ship or a submarine. The missile is approximately 18 feet (5.5 m) in length.[10] It can travel hundreds of miles and explode within 50 feet (15 m) of its programmed target.

THE NAVY'S BUDGET
FISCAL YEAR 2014

Military Personnel	$45.4 billion
Procurement	$43.5 billion
Operations and Maintenance	$48.5 billion
Research and Development	$16 billion
Infrastructure	$2.3 billion
Total (numbers do not add exactly due to rounding)	$155.8 billion[11]

ARMED SERVICES BUDGET
FISCAL YEAR 2014

Army	$129.7 billion
Navy/Marines	$155.8 billion
Air Force	$144.4 billion[12]
Coast Guard	$9.8 billion[13]

CHAPTER SIX
NAVY CAREERS

There are far more jobs and career positions within the US Navy than simply being a sailor. The navy employs a diverse range of people for a host of different jobs. As a group, active-duty sailors are called the operating forces. Sailors can be either enlisted, meaning they joined the

Thousands of young people commit to join the navy each year, most entering as enlisted personnel.

navy without special training, or officers, meaning they have attended the US Naval Academy or another officer-training program.

People may join the US Navy by enlisting after receiving a high school diploma. They can become officers by graduating from college and then enlisting, going through the US Naval Academy, or joining the Naval Reserve Officer Training Corps (NROTC) at a civilian college or university.

BELLS AND WATCHES

Time onboard a navy ship is broken into four-hour periods known as watches. The bell is rung every half hour to alert sailors how far they are through the watch. One half hour into the watch, the bell is rung once. After another half hour, the bell is rung twice. This continues every half hour until the bell is rung eight times, signifying the end of the watch. The morning watch begins at 4:30 a.m. The forenoon watch bell rings out at 8:30 a.m. At 12:30 p.m., the afternoon watch commences. The next watch is split into what is called the first dog watch, which begins at 4:30 p.m., and the second dog watch, which starts at 6:30 p.m. The first watch takes place at 10:30 p.m., followed by the mid watch at 12:30 a.m.

Enlisted sailors are the general workforce of the US Navy. The types of jobs they hold are often similar to those held by civilians. Some sailors work with electronics. Others are trained to be mechanics. There are computer science experts, chefs, law enforcement personnel, and firemen. But unlike in the civilian world, these sailors are trained to perform their jobs on ships at sea.

AVIATION AND FLIGHT SUPPORT

Aviation is an integral part of the US Navy. Along with the presence the navy has on the water, it needs assistance and support in the sky. Naval pilots must have a four-year college degree. Training is extensive. After graduating from the Naval Academy, an NROTC program, or Officer

Candidate School, candidates go through a six-week course at Naval Aviation Schools Command in Pensacola, Florida, followed by primary flight training and advanced training.

But piloting an airplane or helicopter is not the only job in the aviation field. The navy relies upon flight support to keep its pilots flying. Aviation mechanics, air traffic controllers, weapons technicians, and many other positions keep airplanes and helicopters working properly.

Air traffic controllers maintain the safe, orderly flow of air traffic around aircraft carriers. They interpret data on radar screens to plot aircraft positions and tell pilots when they are clear for takeoff and landing. Because air traffic controllers are responsible for making split-second decisions and must be knowledgeable about aircraft, weather, and other factors, it is considered a challenging career.

Other crew members serve as loadmasters, supervising the loading, rigging, and weight of cargo. They also work with pilots to complete preflight equipment

TOPGUN

The US Navy Strike Fighter Tactics Instructor Program teaches select naval aviators and flight officers special tactics and techniques. The students then teach what they learned to their units upon their return. The program, more commonly called TOPGUN, was established in 1969. It was developed to address the shortcomings of air-to-air combat training during the Vietnam War. TOPGUN has become widely known through the 1986 film *Top Gun* starring Tom Cruise.

checks. Mechanics and machinists keep airplanes, hydraulics, power plants, and all other equipment in working condition. College degrees are not required for these positions.

Gunner's mates have the job of keeping their ship's weapons working and firing them in battle. They test and inspect ammunition and missiles. They must know how the guns work and how to fix them. They are trained to aim and fire guns at enemy aircraft and warships.

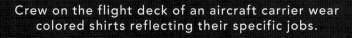
Crew on the flight deck of an aircraft carrier wear colored shirts reflecting their specific jobs.

Though they also use advanced computers and navigational technology, many navy navigators still employ paper maps and charts.

Navigators use naval maps, charts, global positioning systems, and other technology to determine the ship's location and plot a course to its destination. Navigators use radar to locate objects and ships and track them in order to avoid a collision. Navigators are responsible for guiding the ship around shallow areas and away from land.

The navy's size and complexity mean that it requires considerable office and administrative support. These positions do not require a four-year degree. They include such jobs as career counseling, interviewing personnel, recording aircraft maintenance, serving as chaplains, and writing letters and reports.

MEDICAL CORPS, DENTAL CORPS, AND NURSE CORPS

Doctors, nurses, and dentists serve in the US Navy at more than 250 medical facilities around the globe and on board large warships and hospital ships such as the *Mercy* and the *Comfort*. The navy helps pay for their medical education. Doctors specialize in a particular field, such as surgery, neurology, or orthopedic medicine. They then work at military medical facilities on shore, at sea, or in the field. These doctors take care of navy personnel and also offer medical assistance during humanitarian aid efforts.

Navy dentists also specialize in particular areas of dentistry. They perform checkups, fill cavities, and offer preventive care. They care for navy personnel, the families of service members, and people living in parts of the world where dental care is not readily available.

Navy nurses also work to keep navy personnel well. They help navy doctors care for sick patients, assist with surgeries, and work onboard the *Mercy* and the *Comfort*.

The *Comfort*, like the *Mercy*, is a massive floating hospital.

ENGINEERING AND SCIENCES

Officers holding degrees in civil, mechanical, or electrical engineering may serve as part of the US Navy Civil Engineer Corps. These engineers help manage contracts between the navy and civilian contractors that build ships and equipment. These contracts are often worth millions of dollars, so the navy relies heavily upon its engineers to prevent mistakes that can lead to delays and wasted funding.

Naval engineers oversee base maintenance, construction and repair projects, and public works plans.

Seabees worked alongside the citizens of the Pacific island nation of Vanuatu on civil construction projects in 2011.

They also manage the building of airfields, bridges, and ports.

SEABEES

The Navy Construction Battalion (CB) completes many construction projects every year. Better known as the Seabees, members of the CB are the construction crew of the navy. Their work building roads, landing strips, and bases in war-torn areas helps operating forces do their jobs more easily. The motto of the Seabees is "We Build, We Fight."[1]

Seabees do not need college degrees. Training and service in the CB can translate into credits toward a college degree later. Seabees may go on to pursue civilian careers in such fields as carpentry, plumbing, surveying, and heavy equipment operation.

THE NAVY'S WORKER BEES

The nickname Seabees comes from the shortened version of Construction Battalion—CB. These units bulldoze, pave, and build naval facilities all over the world. During the Vietnam War, Seabees constructed camps for special forces, built schools, and repaired infrastructure. They also acted as support for marines, building aircraft facilities, roads, and bridges. Following the Vietnam War, the Seabees were deployed to repair bases in Puerto Rico, Japan, Guam, Greece, Sicily, and Spain. The Seabees were present in the Middle East throughout the Iraq War, constructing bases for US and allied forces in the midst of war zones.

CHAPTER SEVEN
US NAVY SPECIAL FORCES

A select number of people in the navy work in special
forces units. Conducting top-secret missions behind
enemy lines, jumping out of helicopters to rescue people
from freezing waters, and diving beneath ships to clear
explosives are just a few of the tasks performed by navy

Special forces frequently take on extreme, high-intensity missions.

special forces. These jobs are for the elite few who are at the peak of their skills and physical performance. The qualifications for these units are very demanding, and training is very intense.

NAVY SEALS

The Navy SEAL motto is, "The Only Easy Day Was Yesterday."[1] Their name is short for Navy Sea, Air, and Land forces. The navy describes their mission as requiring "highly specialized, intensely challenging warfare capabilities that are beyond the means of standard military forces."[2] In short, the Navy SEALs are ready to do what no one else can do.

In order to prepare SEALs for any situation imaginable, the navy puts them through physically and mentally demanding training. A college degree is not required. Currently, women are not allowed to apply to the Navy SEAL program.

SEALs must be able to adapt to any environment. They are trained to work in deserts, mountains, forests, jungles, arctic areas, and cities. Initial training lasts more than 12 months. During this time, SEALs are trained in land warfare, combat diving, underwater demolition, parachute jumping, and physical

A PHYSICAL CHALLENGE

In order to qualify for acceptance into the US Navy SEAL training program, applicants must pass tough physical requirements. Successful applicants will typically beat the minimum requirements, which are:

- Swimming 500 yards (457 m) in 12 minutes and 30 seconds
- Performing 50 push-ups in 2 minutes
- Performing 50 sit-ups in 2 minutes
- Performing 10 pull-ups in 2 minutes
- Running 1.5 miles (2.4 km) in 10 minutes and 30 seconds[3]

conditioning. This is followed by an additional 18 months of specialized training.

When a SEAL completes training, the duties available vary widely. Some SEALs, such as those in the elite unit commonly called SEAL Team Six, capture or kill high-ranking terrorists around the world. Others are trained to carry out underwater reconnaissance and destroy beach obstacles before soldiers land. Some SEALs carry out small-scale precision missions in the context of a wider battle featuring normal forces.

AVIATION RESCUE SWIMMERS

Navy aviation rescue swimmers are called upon to save lives. They jump from helicopters to rescue crew members in frigid waters, aid stranded hurricane victims, or rappel to remote aircraft crash sites to rescue survivors. The aviation rescue swimmer motto is "So Others May Live," and when lives are on the line, these brave men and women

OPERATION NEPTUNE SPEAR

Among SEAL Team Six's most famous missions was the May 2011 killing of terrorist leader Osama bin Laden. Bin Laden, who was responsible for the September 11, 2001, terrorist attacks against the United States, was discovered to be hiding out in a compound in Abbottabad, Pakistan. Using stealth helicopters previously unknown to the public, approximately two dozen SEALs silently entered Pakistan and landed at the compound in the early morning of May 2. They entered the building, found bin Laden, and killed him. The SEALs removed his body, along with documents and hard drives. One helicopter, damaged during the raid, was intentionally destroyed at the compound. No SEALs were injured or killed.

Rescue swimmers train in highly realistic conditions.

are ready to go into harm's way.[4] Aviation rescue swimmers belong to one of the top emergency response units in the world. Unlike navy search and rescue swimmers, who are attached to a ship, aviation rescue swimmers operate out of aircraft.

Candidates commit to nearly two years of training that includes skills such as lifesaving techniques, water and land survival, and flight safety. Some enlisted rescue swimmers continue with training, attending Advanced Rescue Swimmer School, where they learn rescue techniques for use in swift-moving waters, rough seas, and caves.

NAVY DIVERS

Navy divers journey into the depths of the ocean to accomplish difficult tasks. They perform salvage operations on shipwrecks, assist with construction and demolition projects, carry out search and rescue missions, and do many other jobs.

Navy divers specialize in particular fields. Salvage and recovery divers locate and retrieve wreckage, clear harbors and waterways, and perform underwater repairs. Deep submergence divers pursue research and conduct classified missions far below the surface. Ship husbandry divers are tasked with inspecting and repairing ships and submarines. Saturation divers are trained to live at extreme depths for several weeks at a time while carrying out salvage operations and other deep-sea work.

"We Dive the World Over" is the motto of navy divers.[5] Traveling the world, these specialists encounter

THE FIRST AFRICAN-AMERICAN NAVY DIVER

Carl Brashear became the US Navy's first African-American navy diver in 1953. Brashear not only overcame the obstacle of racism to earn the title of navy diver, but also overcame extraordinary odds after he lost his left leg while onboard the *Hoist* in 1966. Wearing an artificial leg, Brashear underwent therapy and an exercise program that included carrying weights on his back to prepare him for the burden of the scuba tanks. Against all odds, Brashear was eventually promoted to the rank of Master Diver.

every possible undersea environment, from tropical to frigid. Both men and women are eligible to become divers, and a college degree is not necessary.

SPECIAL WARFARE COMBATANT-CRAFT CREWMEN

While the military relies on the SEALs to carry out the toughest missions possible, the SEALs rely on Special Warfare Combatant-Craft Crewmen (SWCC) to provide them with mission support. They operate primarily on rivers and coastlines, collaborating with other special forces units. They are, as their motto states, "The Quiet Professionals."[6]

SWCCs offer support by quickly transporting SEALs in shallow water where larger ships are unable to go. They also attack enemy ships, maintain weapons systems, and provide communications support. Only men may apply for the SWCC program, and a college degree is not required.

EXPLOSIVE ORDNANCE DISPOSAL TECHNICIANS

Wherever explosive threats may lurk, whether on land or in the water, Navy Explosive Ordnance Disposal (EOD) Technicians are ready to handle dangerous situations. EOD Technicians put their lives on the line to respond to unexploded weapons. They demolish these weapons using specialized techniques, locate and identify underwater explosives, support the fleet by clearing mines, and work with the latest technology to safely and remotely disable unsafe explosives. Navy EOD Technicians also help protect high-ranking officials and provide security at large international events, such as the Olympic Games.

The US Navy special forces are not for everyone. However, for the elite people who have the mental and physical discipline to succeed in them, the rewards stretch beyond the time spent in the navy. Veterans of special forces units find that their highly specialized skills, self-determination, and loyalty make them highly sought-after in the civilian job market.

EOD Technicians train to quickly board ships from helicopters.

The navy is often on the cutting edge of new technology.

CHAPTER EIGHT
LIFE IN THE US NAVY

While a career in the US Navy can offer opportunities for travel and adventure, there is a lot more to naval service than that. There are many things to consider before deciding to join any branch of the military. One key thing to think about is the qualifications needed to join.

To enlist in the US Navy, applicants must be between the ages of 17 and 34. They must also be a US citizen or permanent resident of the United States. People who enlist must have a high school diploma or receive a general equivalency diploma. Finally, applicants must pass drug screenings and have a clean criminal history.

Navy recruiters can answer many of the questions that arise when a person is considering enlisting. They are trained to discuss options and expectations and determine if a career in the navy is a good fit for an individual. They can also talk with family members and parents who might have questions or concerns.

Once a candidate decides to enlist in the navy, he or she must provide several pieces of information, including medical records, a birth certificate, a high school diploma, and other documents.

Upon filling out the paperwork, the next step is taking the Armed Services Vocational Aptitude Battery (ASVAB), a two-hour exam designed to help pinpoint an individual's strengths and weaknesses. It tests basic academic knowledge and gauges whether a person has aptitude in a particular field.

Navy recruits must undergo a physical examination and later pass the Navy Physical Readiness Test. The test consists of push-ups, sit-ups, and a 1.5-mile (2.4 km) timed run. Body composition is also determined. Males cannot have a body fat percentage of more than 22 percent, and females cannot have more than 33 percent. Certain medical conditions can disqualify a person from being accepted into the navy, as can a history of drug or alcohol abuse.

The navy recommends that recruits be in excellent shape before joining and taking the Navy Physical Readiness Test.

Upon completion of the physical exam, a counselor will help a candidate choose a job path based on ASVAB and physical results. Once a recruit settles upon a job, he or she can sign the enlistment contract and take the Oath of Enlistment. The oath is not to be taken lightly, as it binds a person into service with the US Navy for at least the next four years.

TRAINING BEGINS

After taking the Oath of Enlistment, recruits head to boot camp for seven to nine weeks at the Great Lakes Naval Training Center north of Chicago, Illinois. In addition to attending navy classes, each group of recruits trains in conditioning, swimming, marching, drilling, and weaponry. Drill instructors transform recruits into a team of disciplined sailors. Everyone learns the proper names of all parts of the ship, how to send signals with flags, how to identify different ships and aircraft, and the laws of basic seamanship.

Recruits also learn how to deal with emergencies. They are trained to fight fires, escape smoke-filled compartments, and open and close watertight doors. After rigorous training, recruits face a test known as Battle Stations. They confront different simulated scenarios that test their newly gained knowledge. Recruits must work together as a team. Once they have passed, they proceed to the final week of boot camp. They wear their official US Navy uniforms for the first time and celebrate with family and friends as they officially become sailors.

Once basic training is complete, recruits are promoted to seaman apprentices and go on to receive advanced training. After this next round of training, enlisted sailors are ready to begin their naval career. They are given a few days off to return home and be with family and friends before reporting to their first duty station.

BECOMING AN OFFICER

Most officers in the US Navy hold college degrees. Officers may do this by either graduating from college and then joining the navy, or by attending the US Naval Academy in Annapolis, Maryland. Some who attend college take advantage of the NROTC, which allows students to attend college while taking naval courses. The NROTC program pays for a person's college tuition. Upon graduation, the graduate commits to being an officer in the US Navy for a minimum of five years. Officers take on more responsibility than enlisted people. They are also paid more.

Those who attend the US Naval Academy in Annapolis prepare to become professional officers in the US Navy and

THE MISSION OF THE UNITED STATES NAVAL ACADEMY

According to the US Naval Academy, the institution's mission is:

To develop midshipmen morally, mentally, and physically and to imbue them with the highest ideals of duty, honor and loyalty in order to graduate leaders who are dedicated to a career of naval service and have potential for future development in mind and character to assume the highest responsibilities of command, citizenship, and government.[1]

Marine Corps. Students attend the academy for four years, graduate with a bachelor of science degree, and become midshipmen on active duty in the US Navy or Second Lieutenants in the Marine Corps.

After boot camp, those with college degrees attend Officer Candidate School or Officer Development School. Officer Candidate School is at Naval Station Newport in Rhode Island. Twelve weeks of training prepare candidates to become officers. Candidates take classes on academic subjects, leadership, and military training. People who are already officers and are pursuing specific courses of study, such as nuclear engineering or medicine, attend Officer Development School at the same location.

DAILY LIFE IN THE NAVY

Day to day life in the navy differs greatly depending upon which job a person does. Ships typically go to sea for ten to fourteen days each month for training operations, but extended missions can last up to nine months. Most hours of the day are spent performing one's job duties. Free time is spent exercising, writing e-mails home, playing cards or games with friends, or taking extra classes and studying.

Like civilians, navy personnel are entitled to time off, which is called leave. However, service members cannot take leave whenever they want. They must first receive approval from commanding officers. Additionally, wartime

A DAY AT THE
NAVAL ACADEMY

6:30 a.m.: A special instruction period for first-year students begins.
7:00 a.m.: Morning meal formation
7:15 a.m.: Morning meal
7:55 a.m.: Academics, consisting of four class periods of 50 minutes each
12:05 p.m.: Noon meal formation
12:10 p.m.: Noon meal
12:50 p.m.: Company training time
1:30 p.m.: Fifth and sixth class periods
3:45 p.m.: Athletics and extracurricular activities are held. Drills and parades occur twice a week in the fall and spring.
6:30 p.m.: Evening meal
8:00 p.m.: Study time

necessity might make it difficult for service members to take leave. In the event of a family emergency, navy personnel may be granted emergency leave to return home.

Navy personnel stationed on bases will typically live in barracks, dormitories that provide basic living needs. Those with spouses or families generally live in apartments or houses on the base or nearby. Housing allowances help cover the cost of furniture and utilities. Sailors who are stationed on ships and submarines are assigned to a berthing area where they have their own bunk and a locker for storing personal belongings.

BENEFITS OF NAVAL SERVICE

In addition to pride in serving one's country, there are other benefits to joining the navy. The US Navy has a world-class training program in a wide range of skills. Additionally, it offers both exciting careers and job stability to enlisted personnel or officers. Many people get to see parts of the world and different cultures they probably would not have the opportunity to experience without

LIFE ON A SUBMARINE

Only 6 percent of all navy personnel serve aboard a submarine.[2] Submariners have to be versatile, able to perform highly technical work, and have strong teamwork skills. Training and preparation generally take one year before candidates earn their Submarine Warfare Insignia pins. Submariners live in cramped quarters and must be ready to employ expertise in areas such as damage control, propulsion, electronic equipment, navigation, and combat systems.

naval service. For those who are attracted to being on the water, the navy offers a host of opportunities on boats and bodies of water of all kinds.

Some people make a full career out of service in the US Navy. Others serve their four to six years and then reenter civilian life. Some opt to serve more years than their initial enlistment requires and go part-time in the US Navy Reserve. All who serve at least 20 years are eligible for full retirement pay and health benefits.

Serving in the US Navy Reserve requires service for at least a few days a month. In return, reservists earn basic pay and are still able to pursue a civilian career. Navy reservists may be called up for active duty in times of war or other crises.

Upon completion of navy service, former officers and sailors reenter civilian life with the benefit of top-notch training, knowledge, and experience. Navy doctors and nurses continue their medical careers at civilian hospitals and clinics. Navy pilots often pursue careers flying for commercial or private airlines. Navy mechanics, photographers, computer experts, human resources personnel, food workers, and others are able to translate their experiences into similar civilian jobs.

Entering the US Navy provides world-class training, knowledge, and experiences that will give an individual a great advantage when the time comes to reenter civilian

People who join the navy often have the opportunity to see places they might not otherwise visit.

The US Navy has a rich tradition of honoring its veterans.

life. Additionally, the discipline, physical fitness, and mental alertness honed by a naval career can contribute to a healthier and richer life long after one's service in the US Navy is over.

RANKS

Enlisted Titles

Seaman Recruit
<-········· Seaman Apprentice
Seaman
Petty Officer 3rd Class
Petty Officer 2nd Class
Petty Officer 1st Class ·····>
Chief Petty Officer
Senior Chief Petty Officer
Master Chief Petty Officer
Master Chief Petty Officer of the Navy

Officers

Chief Warrant Officer 2
Chief Warrant Officer 3
Chief Warrant Officer 4
Chief Warrant Officer 5
<················· Ensign
Lieutenant Junior Grade
Lieutenant
Lieutenant Commander
Commander
Captain ················>
Rear Admiral (lower half)
Rear Admiral (upper half)
Vice Admiral
Admiral

TIMELINE

1775

The Continental Congress establishes the Continental navy on October 13.

1798

The US Department of the Navy is established on April 30.

1801–1805

US Navy vessels are deployed to the Barbary Coast where they defend US merchant vessels during the First Barbary War.

1812

The United States declares war against the United Kingdom on June 18, launching the War of 1812.

1845

The United States Naval Academy is founded in Annapolis, Maryland.

1861–1865

The American Civil War pits the US Navy against Confederate ships, including the armored *Virginia*.

1898

On May 1, Commodore George Dewey defeats a Spanish fleet in the Philippines.

1917–1918

The United States fights alongside the United Kingdom during World War I. Navy convoys protect and supply troops going to and serving in Europe.

1941

On December 7, the US naval base at Pearl Harbor, Hawaii, is bombed in a surprise Japanese attack, leading to the US entry into World War II.

1964–1973

During the Vietnam War, the US Navy patrols rivers and launches air strikes from carriers.

1991

US Navy aircraft fly missions against enemy targets during the Persian Gulf War.

2004

After the December 26 tsunami, the US Navy deploys ships to come to the aid of survivors in Indonesia.

ESSENTIAL FACTS

DATE OF FOUNDING
October 13, 1775

MOTTO
No official motto, but
Non sibi sed patriae
(Not self but country) is
sometimes known as the
unofficial motto.

PERSONNEL (2013)
53,000 officers
265,000 enlisted members
4,000 midshipmen at the US Naval Academy
100,000 in the ready reserve
200,000 civilian employees

ROLE
The US Navy defends the coasts of the United States.
Using its vast fleets of ships and aircraft, it also
projects power throughout the world's oceans. In
addition to its military role, the navy also participates
in humanitarian missions that leverage its impressive
logistical capabilities.

SIGNIFICANT MISSIONS

The fight between the *Monitor* and the *Virginia* during the Civil War marked the first battle between ironclad ships and helped propel the craft of shipbuilding forward following the war.

The Battle of Midway during World War II represented the turning point of the war in the Pacific.

WELL-KNOWN NAVY MEMBERS

John Paul Jones was a famous Continental navy captain during the American Revolutionary War.

David Farragut won important victories on the Mississippi River during the Civil War.

Chester Nimitz served as a fleet admiral during World War II. A class of aircraft carrier was named after him.

QUOTE

"I have not yet begun to fight!" —*John Paul Jones*

GLOSSARY

AMPHIBIOUS
Operating on both land and water.

BARRACKS
Buildings where soldiers live.

BATTALION
A large unit or group of troops.

CIVILIAN
A person who is not a member of the military.

COMMISSION
To order a ship into active service.

CONVOY
A group of ships traveling together for protection.

CORSAIR
A privateer of the Barbary Coast.

FLEET
A group of military ships that move and work together.

FRIGATE
Historically, a light boat that was propelled by oars and later by sails; today, a ship that is smaller than a destroyer.

MARITIME
Of or relating to navigation or commerce on the sea.

MUNITIONS
Ammunition.

RAPPEL
To descend from higher ground or an aircraft using a rope.

RECONNAISSANCE
Scouting or surveying, especially in wartime.

SONAR
A device that uses sound waves to locate objects under the water.

SQUADRON
A naval unit consisting of multiple vessels.

STALEMATE
A contest or battle in which neither side is a clear winner.

STARBOARD
The right side of a ship or boat as you face the front, or bow, of the vessel.

TSUNAMI
A large, destructive tidal wave produced when the ground shifts, such as during an earthquake or volcanic eruption.

ADDITIONAL RESOURCES

SELECTED BIBLIOGRAPHY

Cutler, Thomas J. *A Sailor's History of the US Navy.* Annapolis, MD: Naval Institute P, 2005. Print.

Toll, Ian W. *Six Frigates: The Epic History of the Founding of the US Navy.* New York: Norton, 2008. Print.

FURTHER READINGS

Hamilton, John. *Aircraft Carriers.* Minneapolis, MN: Abdo, 2013. Print.

Marciniak, Kristin. *Navy SEALs.* Minneapolis, MN: Abdo, 2013. Print.

WEBSITES

To learn more about Essential Library of the US Military, visit **booklinks.abdopublishing.com**. These links are routinely monitored and updated to provide the most current information available.

PLACES TO VISIT

NATIONAL MUSEUM OF THE US NAVY

Washington Navy Yard
805 Kidder Breese Street SE
Washington, DC 20374
202-433-4882
http://www.history.navy.mil/branches/org8-1.htm

See historic documents and artifacts, models of famous ships, and artwork commemorating the US Navy at this official museum.

UNITED STATES NAVAL ACADEMY VISITOR CENTER

52 King George Street
Annapolis, MD 21402
410-293-8687
http://www.usnabsd.com/for-visitors/public-tours

The visitor's center at the US Naval Academy gives civilians a chance to see the school, including such historic sights as the crypt of John Paul Jones in the chapel.

SOURCE NOTES

CHAPTER 1. SAILING TO THE RESCUE

1. "2004 December 26 Earthquake Details." *Earthquake Hazards Program*. USGS, 8 July 2013. Web. 28 Mar. 2014.

2. "The Deadliest Tsunami in History?" *National Geographic News*. National Geographic, 7 Jan. 2005. Web. 28 Mar. 2014.

3. Dan Vergano. "Japan's Tsunami Waves Top Historic Heights." *USA Today*. USA Today, 25 Apr. 2011. Web. 10 Nov. 2013.

4. Bruce A. Elleman. "Waves of Hope: The US Navy's Response to the Tsunami in Northern Indonesia." *Naval War College*. US Navy, Feb. 2007. Web. 1 Apr. 2014.

5. "US Navy Relief Efforts after the Indian Ocean Tsunami, 26 December 2004." *Naval History and Heritage Command*. US Navy, 10 May 2007. Web. 28 Mar. 2014.

6. Ibid.

7. "Patient Care." *Command Facilities*. US Navy, n.d. Web. 10 Nov. 2013.

8. Ibid.

9. "US Navy Relief Efforts after the Indian Ocean Tsunami, 26 December 2004." *Naval History and Heritage Command*. US Navy, 10 May 2007. Web. 28 Mar. 2014.

10. Ibid.

11. "Typhoon Haiyan Death Toll Jumps to 5,235 in Philippines." *CNN*. CNN, 22 Nov. 2013. Web. 26 Nov. 2013.

12. "Typhoon Haiyan: Philippines Defends Aid Response." *BBC News*. BBC, 13 Nov. 2013. Web. 26 Nov. 2013.

CHAPTER 2. A NAVY FOR A NEW COUNTRY

1. Robert Hodierne. "Navy, United States." *World Book Advanced*. World Book, 2014. Web. 11 Nov. 2013.

2. "'I Have Not Yet Begun to Fight!': The Story of John Paul Jones." *Naval History and Heritage Command*. US Navy, n.d. Web. 28 Mar. 2014.

3. Captain Daniel J. Carrison. *The United States Navy*. New York: Praeger, 1968. Print. 8.

4. Jeremy Black. "A British View of the Naval War of 1812." *US Naval Institute*. US Naval Institute, Aug. 2008. Web. 28 Mar. 2014.

5. Captain Daniel J. Carrison. *The United States Navy*. New York: Praeger, 1968. Print. 12.

6. Edgar Stanton Maclay. *A History of the United States Navy from 1775 to 1893, Volume I*. New York: D. Appleton, 1893. Print. vi.

CHAPTER 3. A NAVAL POWERHOUSE

1. Robert Hodierne. "Navy, United States." *World Book Advanced*. World Book, 2014. Web. 11 Nov. 2013.

2. Captain Daniel J. Carrison. *The United States Navy*. New York: Praeger, 1968. Print. 17–18.

3. Allen Grove. "Annapolis Profile." *College Admissions*. About.com, 2014. Web. 28 Mar. 2014.

4. Captain Daniel J. Carrison. *The United States Navy*. New York: Praeger, 1968. Print. 22.

5. Stephen Howarth. *To Shining Sea: A History of the United States Navy 1775–1991*. New York: Random, 1991. Print. 331.

6. Paul W. Doerr. "Pearl Harbor." *World Book Advanced*. World Book, 2014. Web. 24 Nov. 2013.

7. "Pearl Harbor." *Military.com*. Military.com, 2014. Web. 28 Mar. 2014.

CHAPTER 4. THE ROLE OF THE US NAVY

1. "MPCON Minute—Navy's Mission Statement." *US Navy*. US Navy, 28 Jan. 2001. Web. 28 Mar. 2014.

2. "US Naval History and Rules." *Military.com*. Military.com, n.d. Web. 1 Dec. 2013.

3. "US Naval History and Rules." *Military.com*. Military.com, n.d. Web. 1 Dec. 2013.

4. "Navy Bases." *Military Bases*. Military Bases, n.d. Web. 28 Mar. 2014.

5. "Bases." *US Navy*. US Navy, n.d. Web. 28 Mar. 2014.

6. "70% Want Navy to Protect US, Not Be 'Global Force for Good.'" *Rasmussen Reports*. Rasmussen Reports, 5 Feb. 2013. Web. 28 Mar. 2014.

7. "US Navy Partnerships: An International Maritime Force." *Navy Live*. US Navy, 28 June 2012. Web. 12 Dec. 2013.

CHAPTER 5. VESSELS OF THE US NAVY

1. "Status of the Navy." *US Navy*. US Navy, 28 Mar. 2014. Web. 28 Mar. 2014.

2. "Aircraft Carriers-CVN." *US Navy Fact File*. US Navy, 20 Nov. 2013. Web. 1 Apr. 2014.

3. Ibid.

4. Ibid.

5. Ronald O'Rourke. "Navy Virginia (SSN-774) Class Attack Submarine Procurement: Background and Issues for Congress." *Congressional Research Service*. Congressional Research Service, 24 Mar. 2014. Web. 1 Apr. 2014.

6. "Virginia Class Attack Submarine – SSN." *Military.com*. Military.com, 2014. Web. 1 Apr. 2014.

7. "F/A-18 Hornet." *Military Analysis Network*. Federation of American Scientists, 25 Apr. 2000. Web. 2 Apr. 2014.

8. "MK 75 – 76mm/62 Caliber Gun." *US Navy Fact File*. US Navy, 15 Nov. 2013. Web. 1 Apr. 2014.

9. "Trident Fleet Ballistic Missile." *US Navy Fact File*. US Navy, 17 Jan. 2009. Web. 1 Apr. 2014.

10. "Tomahawk Cruise Missile." *US Navy Fact File*. US Navy, 23 Apr. 2010. Web. 1 Apr. 2014.

11. "Department of the Navy FY 2014 President's Budget." *US Navy*. US Navy, 10 Apr. 2013. Web. 2 Apr. 2014.

12. "Summary of the DOD Fiscal Year 2014 Budget Proposal." *US Department of Defense*. US Department of Defense, n.d. Web. 2 Apr. 2014.

13. "Fiscal Year 2014 Congressional Justification." *US Coast Guard*. US Coast Guard, n.d. Web. 2 Apr. 2014.

CHAPTER 6. NAVY CAREERS

1. "Construction." *US Navy*. US Navy, n.d. Web. 1 Apr. 2014.

CHAPTER 7. US NAVY SPECIAL FORCES

1. "Navy SEALs (Sea, Air & Land)." *US Navy.* US Navy, n.d. Web. 1 Apr. 2014.
2. Ibid.
3. Ibid.
4. "Aviation Rescue Swimmer (AIRR)." *US Navy.* US Navy, n.d. Web. 1 Apr. 2014.
5. "Navy Diver." *US Navy.* US Navy, n.d. Web. 10 Dec. 2013.
6. "Special Warfare Combatant-Craft Crewman (SWCC)." *US Navy.* US Navy, n.d. Web. 10 Dec. 2013.

CHAPTER 8. LIFE IN THE US NAVY

1. "United States Naval Academy 2017 Class Portrait." *US Naval Academy.* US Navy, n.d. Web. 1 Apr. 2014.
2. "Life on a Sub." *US Navy.* US Navy, n.d. Web. 12 Dec. 2013.

INDEX